IMAGES OF ENGLAND

KEYNSHAM

IMAGES OF ENGLAND

KEYNSHAM

BARBARA LOWE
AND MARGARET WHITEHEAD

TEMPUS

Frontispiece: A symbol of twentieth-century Keynsham, this 1930s advertisement shows a typical *Just William* schoolboy ready to spend his pocket money on a Chocolate Cream bar. In 1928, the Fry's Chocolate Cream advertisement featured Peter Paul, a 'desperate pirate', who was the symbol of the eternal boy who loves make-believe and adventure no less than Fry's Cream Tablets.

First published 2003

Tempus Publishing Limited
The Mill, Brimscombe Port,
Stroud, Gloucestershire, GL5 2QG
www.tempus-publishing.com

British Library Cataloguing in Publication Data.
A catalogue record for this book is available from the British Library.

ISBN 0 7524 3095 5

Typesetting and origination by Tempus Publishing Limited.
Printed in Great Britain by Midway Colour Print, Wiltshire.

Contents

Acknowledgements

The authors wish to thank the following, whose photographs have helped to make this book possible.

In particular, we are exceedingly grateful to Messrs Cadbury, Trebor & Bassett for access to, and use of, the extensive J.S. Fry Archive, and to Hugh Evans (GMP Manager) for his friendly, enthusiastic co-operation and help.

Keynsham Scouts, St John Ambulance (Keynsham Division), the British Legion (Keynsham Branch), St John's (Keynsham) Amateur Dramatic Society, Keynsham Charlton WI and the Keynsham Shotokai Karate Club have very kindly provided photographs.

In addition, over the years many people have donated photographs to the Local History Society Archives and we acknowledge the use here of those given by Tony Brown, Roger Clark, Helen Dunford, David Elliott, the late Miss Fox, Brian Harris, Barbara Lowe, Tony Martin, the late R.D. Lanning, M. Tozer, Margaret and Trevor Whitehead.

We are grateful to Somerset Archaeological & Natural History Society for permission to reproduce the dolphin mosaic tracing from Keynsham Roman Villa; to Sue Trude who helped sort and select the 220 pictures and proof-read the text; to Dennis Hill who composed the captions for the Transport chapter, checked the typescript and carried out the general secretarial work involved; and to Peter Godden who provided pictures and information about the Scouts.

Introduction

Modern Keynsham bears scant evidence of its long and important heritage. Fifty years ago it was a thriving market town with an interesting variety of individual shops in the main street, selling essential goods. Keynsham was self-sufficient with trades and tradesmen to fulfil every need, making trips to Bristol and Bath unnecessary.

The buildings were varied and full of character, as were the personalities in them. Progress and modern lifestyle have resulted in the High Street and town centre having few small, specialist shops, and becoming a haven for increasingly automated banks and building societies, cut-price stores, charity shops, large chain outlets and travel agents.

Keynsham has been a political football. In 1894, under Somerset County Council, Keynsham Rural District Council was established to govern surrounding villages, although Keynsham had its own Parish Council responsible for provision and maintenance of local amenities. In 1933, Keynsham and Saltford were amalgamated to form one unit within Bathavon Rural District but, in 1936, they received approval to form Keynsham Urban District Council and elections took place in 1938. This happy situation lasted until 1974 when Keynsham was removed from Somerset to become part of a new district, Wansdyke, within the newly created county of Avon. On the demise of Avon in 1996, Keynsham became part of the unitary authority, Bath and North-East Somerset.

After the Second World War, a decision was made to create homes for thousands of families from Bristol, enlarging the population of Keynsham and Saltford from 4,521 to 20,636 in a comparatively short time. Huge new estates were built, all on greenfield sites – one on the Abbot of Keynsham's Deer Park and another on the old common fields to the east of the River Chew. A bypass was constructed between 1961 and 1966 to relieve High Street congestion, slashing through parkland which had remained undisturbed for 425 years. This area, now Keynsham Memorial Park, had been chosen by the Anglo-Saxons for their high status burial ground and then by William, Second Earl of Gloucester, for the site of a large and important medieval abbey.

The legend of St Keyna turning all Keynsham's serpents to stone arose because the lias limestone bedrock contains fossilised ammonites which resemble coiled snakes. Fossilised plesiosaurs, ichthyosaurs, belemnites and corals – 175 million years old – can be found here. Humans travelling through the area in around 200,000 BC left bifacial flint and chert axes in the river terrace gravels. Mesolithic people hunted small game here and Neolithic farmers left behind flint scrapers, polished flint and quartz dolerite axes. Colonists from the Low Country and Rhineland occupied the district, leaving Beaker burial sites at Corston. The Romans certainly found our area very favourable, particularly the Keynsham Hams.

The mills, so busy for over 800 years, successively processing corn, wool, cotton, hemp, brass, steel and dyewoods have been dismantled and redeveloped. Other important industries were lime burning, quarrying, growing willow for basket-making, woad and teasel farming for the fulling process, and agriculture. More recent industries have included the manufacture of Glauber's salt, ammonium chloride, soap, paint, waterproof cement and paper – all have died. No one could be blamed for failing to realise that Keynsham had such a valuable heritage, when meagre vestiges are all that remain.

Education was always well provided for and, fortunately, is still, but we have lost our 900 year-old right to hold petty sessions for the hundred. The magistrates court, where quarter sessions were held, and the Victorian police station have gone whilst the present police station is no longer fully manned. Keynsham once had its own gas company, its own electric light and power company, its own electric telegraph, its own telephone exchange, its own postal sorting office – but all have been taken away from us. Local folk bemoan the fact that Keynsham has lost its identity.

The railway put Keynsham on the map in 1840, being on the main line from Bristol to London. The station grew to become Keynsham and Somerdale until the Beeching axe fell. All our station buildings were destroyed in 1970, including the station-master's house, and even the footbridge was sold. Some trains stop here still, but these are becoming less and less frequent.

The coming of Fry's factory in 1922 provided work for over 2,000 people, thus reviving Keynsham's prosperity. Not only was the company an ideal employer, providing pleasant surroundings and leisure facilities for its workers and their families, but it cared about the environment. Two Roman coffins, a small house and a well, discovered during factory construction, were archaeologically investigated. The well was preserved *in situ* and the small house reconstructed near the factory's main entrance gates. A small museum was built to house the artefacts recovered. The company contributed to the excavation of the large courtyard villa under the town cemetery at Durley Hill and to the preservation of portions of mosaic flooring found there. Modern Keynsham has virtually no manufacturing industry other than Cadbury's (formerly Fry's) Chocolate.

With a continuing increase in population has come higher levels of road traffic. The centre of the town has traffic-calming devices and several car parks. Commuters seeking to avoid parking charges leave their cars in residential side streets. Households with three or four cars are not uncommon and many front gardens have been sacrificed for hardstanding. On the outskirts of the town, large signs proclaim: 'Keynsham, Historic Market Town'. The Abbot of Keynsham was granted a charter in 1303 for an annual three-day fair and a weekly Thursday market. Both were discontinued long ago. From the end of 2002 until September 2003, a few stalls selling miscellaneous goods assembled on the town centre forecourt each Friday. Keynsham is still regarded as a good place to live and many residents, both old and new, feel it is a place with a community spirit. They care about the town and are prepared to fight to preserve what little is left. A local businessman has recently renovated shops in Temple Street and developed a very attractive courtyard of small individual shops and businesses. Play facilities for the young are excellent and a number of playing fields cater for team games. The riverside walk from Dapps Hill to below Abbey Park is a haven for pedestrians and wildlife. The trees are beautiful and, in spring and summer, flower beds and hanging baskets are a joy to behold. A fifty-acre community woodland has been established on the eastern edge of town.

one

Environment

Keynsham was a small rural town until after the Second World War, but during the 1950s and 1960s thousands of new houses were built, anything old was destroyed and a bypass was carved through the precinct of Keynsham Abbey, visible in the centre of this 1961 picture. Below this, a British Rail train steams into Keynsham and Somerdale Station, a double-decker bus passes over the thirteenth-century stone bridge which divided Somersetshire from Gloucestershire, and Avon Mill to its left was used by E.S. & A. Robinson, paper manufacturers.

Fry's began their move from Bristol to Keynsham in 1922 and by September that year had begun to construct a railway line to link their factory to the main Great Western line at Keynsham Station. The cutting was through the lias rock of which this is an example.

An impressive anticline appeared in the W side of the cutting. Sedimentary rocks were formed by the hardening of layers of material deposited at the bottom or on the shores of seas, rivers and lakes. Many rocks were twisted out of their original positions during the process of upheaval, in this case causing an anticline or inverted v-shape.

This unusual stone was revealed by a local resident digging a sump in his front garden. It appears to be a huge, badly cracked ammonite, covered with concretions.

These ammonites (*bucklandi*) are common in the upper part of the alsatites liasicus zone of the area's limestone and are fossilised, extinct sea creatures closely related to the nautili.

On the Bristol side of Keynsham, the River Avon forms a large u-bend and the very rich meadow land within the bend is known as Keynsham Hams. Until 1914, much of it was divided into strips but, gradually, Fry's purchased the whole area of 220 acres. This is how it looked in 1920. Notice Keynsham Church (bottom left).

Fry's also purchased Cleve Woods on the Gloucestershire side of the Avon. Here, coppicing is taking place in 1930, all by hand, the piles of cut twigs being carried on a two-pronged fork to a bonfire to be burned.

This part of the woods, once Londonderry Farm land, was planted with ash in 1934, but in March 1952 it was re-planted with poplar, beech, sycamore, larch and Scots fir.

In 1940, it was necessary to control wild animals around the chocolate factory. It appears that this team is using some kind of gassing apparatus, perhaps in rabbit burrows.

Fry's factory had grown considerably by 1928 and their products were transported to all parts of the world. Fry's own rail trucks may be seen at the extreme top of the picture, whilst middle left is Keynsham lock.

The lock-keeper, Jackie White, is seen operating the lock gates in April 1932. Water is swirling near the steps below Jackie's cottage as the water in the lock is lowered. The old County Bridge forms the backdrop.

The road bridge over the railway line near the Keynsham and Somerdale Station was widened on both sides. The N side was widened in November 1931 and the other side, shown here, in June 1932. Notice the gorgeous two-seater pram.

Opposite above: The mill was to the north of Chew Bridge. A local artist made these sketches of the last days of the old colour mill on 26 March 1948 and gave them to our society. The mill was demolished soon afterwards.

Opposite below: This sketch was taken from the stone bridge with the sluice gates to the left. The other sketch shows the entrance.

Left: The houses in Chandos Road were built by Fry's for their employees. The road was lined with cherry trees which looked delightful in bloom, as seen here in May 1946. An electric milk float made daily deliveries of glass-bottled milk to all households.

Below: Chew or Downe Mill is thought to have been one of the Domesday mills on the River Chew. It was later used for fulling and, from 1705 until the 1870s, it operated as a brass battery mill. From then until the 1930s, it was used for ochre grinding and was referred to as 'The colour mill in the Memorial Park'.

17

This weir, a 15ft-diameter waterwheel and a few stunted walls are all that remain of the mill today.

Avon Mill, another Domesday mill, ceased operating as a brass-rolling and wire-drawing mill in 1927-28, shortly before this photograph was taken by a local resident. It had eight waterwheels.

The mill was bought by E.S. & A. Robinson, paper manufacturers, and used from 1933 until the 1970s when this picture was taken. In 1963, the firm decided to build a paper mill on open ground next door to the old brass mill. The old mill pond and water courses were later filled in.

This ancient mill site, originally called South Mill, was renamed Albert Mill following rebuilding after a disastrous fire in 1873. It became a woollen mill in the 1770s, then adapted to cotton and flax spinning, returned to corn milling, before being adapted for crushing lime and ochre in 1836. Imported woods were chipped and ground in the dyewood process which continued until 1964. Here the mill building is shown awaiting redevelopment in June 1987.

The weir and water course of the mill has been altered but now forms an attractive feature of the residential development on the site. A waterwheel has been preserved.

The precinct of the old abbey was bought by the local council in 1948 and made into the Memorial Park. This view of the park, including the tree-rimmed spring known locally as 'The Abbot's Fish Pond', was taken from Abbey Park.

The top of Keynsham Church tower is an excellent place from which to view the town. Here, in the 1960s, the council nursery site is immaculate, as are the tennis courts and bowling green.

This picture, from the same viewpoint in 1978, shows a neat bowling green and tennis courts, but the council's garden nursery is derelict and the swathe of the bypass cuts the park in two.

Left: The western side of the park is very popular with young families and the children's play area is well used. Many mothers bring their children who play awhile and then eat their picnic lunches with as much enthusiasm as young Stephanie Lowe.

Below: Not long before the serious floods of July 1968, a new lower park had been designed and laid out in place of the allotments between Temple Street and the River Chew. The floods wrecked it all.

The whole had to be redesigned and today it is a very attractive, peaceful area. The tranquillity is seen in this 1999 photograph.

Younger children love to come here and feed the ever-hungry mallards and pigeons. Young William Lowe was very indignant when a duck snatched bread from his hand and bit his finger.

An attractive sight in spring are the mallard ducks with their tiny ducklings. Some have as many as fourteen, but one wonders how many survive to adulthood.

This is a typical natural hay meadow in Keynsham, showing fiorin and reed grass, meadow foxtail, red clover, great knapweed, ox-eye daisy and meadow vetchling.

Traditionally, Keynsham had a large farming community and up until about 1927 the chief crops were wheat, barley, oats and root crops.

24

Above: Another fodder crop, melilot, was grown here and still may be found wild on waste ground. This was a medieval medicinal herb from which plasters and poultices were made.

Right: The area was once famous for its crops of the rare plant, Bath asparagus (*Ornithogalum pyrenaicum*). This was a delicacy and the unopened flower spikes were sold in Bath market. Wild colonies have established themselves locally.

Orchids are highly specialised for insect pollination and one of the three petals is modified into a conspicuous lip which secretes nectar. This pyramid orchid, growing locally, is one of our prettiest orchids but it has a peculiar odour which some people like, others do not.

Bee orchids are common in calcareous areas and grow on waste land in Keynsham. However, growth is slow, they are hard to transplant and extremely difficult to grow from their minute seeds. Vanilla flavouring is made from the seed pod.

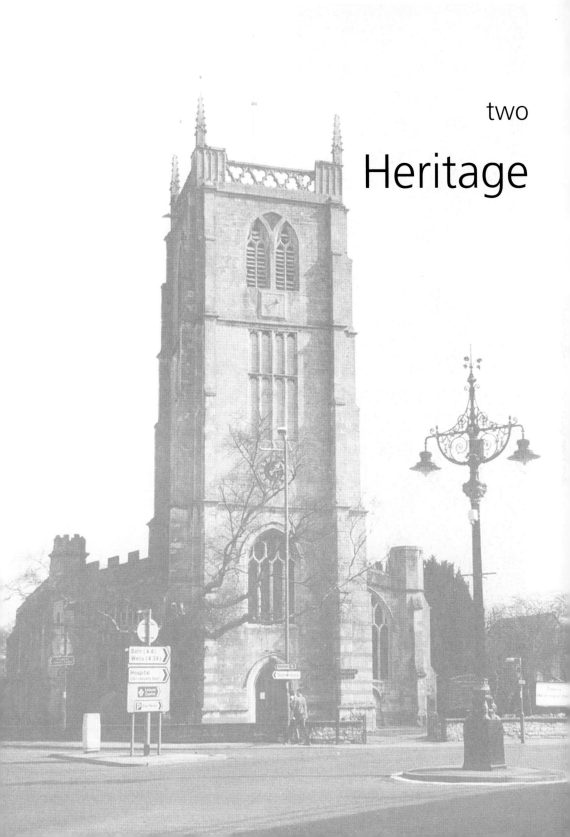

two

Heritage

Whilst a bypass was being cut through the precinct of Keynsham Abbey, three exceptionally well-carved Romanesque ceiling bosses were found. This one, depicting Samson subduing the lion, is the most beautiful.

Flint arrowheads were discovered amongst spoil heaps from an inadvertently destroyed Romano-British settlement on Keynsham Hams. The leaf-shaped one dates from the Neolithic period and the other is a tanged arrowhead.

Right: At Corston, a few miles east of Keynsham, two crouched burials were found in two stone cists, with a beaker in each. This is one of them. Colonists came here from the Low Countries and Rhineland during the Bronze Age, around the second millennium BC.

Below: Whilst excavating for gravel for the foundations of the new Fry's chocolate factory in 1922, two Roman coffins were found side by side, about eighteen inches below ground. They were hollowed out of solid Bath stone, the larger, lead-lined one containing a male, the smaller one, a female.

The foundations of a small Roman house were found during construction of the factory. The remains of this villa were lifted and reconstructed near the main entrance to the factory in October 1930.

Keynsham's large courtyard villa, the remains of which lie under the cemetery at Durley Hill, was partially excavated during 1924-26. The villa had extensive mosaic flooring and this photograph shows part of the geometrical design of the north corridor floor.

Burials had already taken place in the cemetery for over thirty years, so many pavements had been destroyed. However, it proved possible to lift and preserve nine mosaic panels, six of which are illustrated here. The square panels depict, from left to right, Achilles and the maidens, Europa and the bull and Minerva with her reflection in her magic shield.

A close-up showing the detail in the mosaic of one of the birds (perhaps a peacock?) in the front left-hand panel of the previous picture. These six panels were from one of the hexagonal corner rooms of the villa.

Above: Many of the mosaic floors were too damaged to lift, but some were traced in situ and the tracings preserved in the library of the Somerset Archaeological and Natural History Society at Taunton. This tracing of a dolphin and chalice is shown by courtesy of that society.

Left: Keynsham had a high status Anglo-Saxon burial ground in the ninth century and a minster church. This Anglo-Saxon bookclasp (gilded bronze) was found during bypass work in 1964.

Opposite above: Keynsham Abbey was founded in around 1170 and dissolved in 1539. The thirteenth-century seal of the abbey is seen on the right, the seal of Abbot Adam (1280) on the left.

Opposite below: These steps, paved with tiles dated to 1280, led up to a stone altar at the east side of a small south chapel in the abbey.

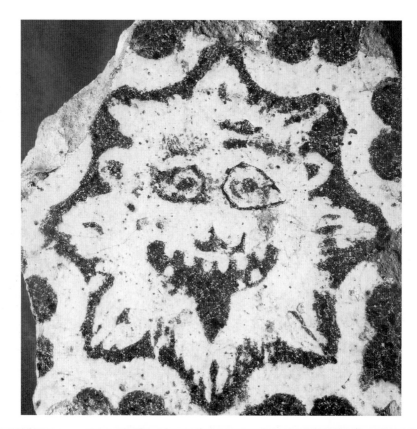

Above: This is how the remains of the abbey look today. Medieval herbs have been planted above the made-up walling of the north cloister and south nave and are tended by volunteers from the Bristol History and Archaeology Society (formerly called the Folk House Archaeological Society).

Opposite above: When viewed upside-down, the 'laughing lion' design on this fourteenth-century floor tile appears to be a wizened old man.

Opposite below: This shows the second of the three ceiling bosses, which probably came from the refectory of the abbey. The four gargoyle-like faces, biting the vaulting ribs, must have looked evil to the canons eating below.

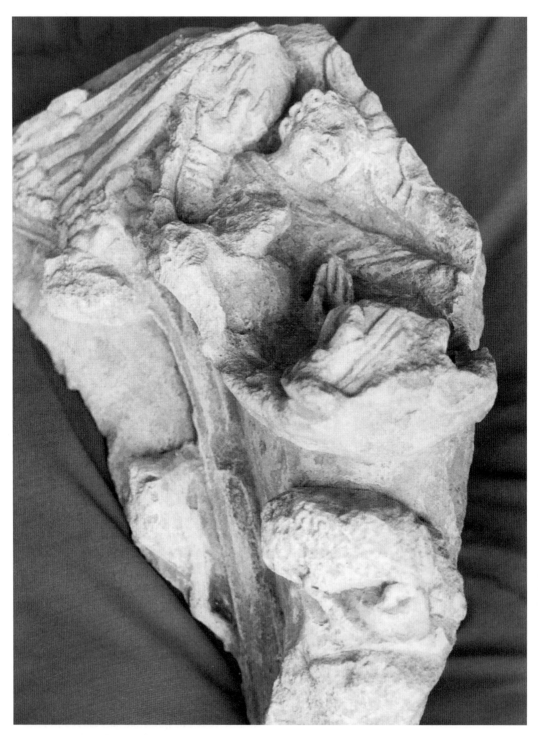

The rubble remains of the destroyed chapter house of the abbey produced fragments of delicately sculptured stone. Perhaps this piece depicts the sacrifice of Isaac. Notice the angels' wings, the curly heads and the lovely, tiny hands.

Above: This Holy water stoup from the abbey church was rescued from a local garden folly, where it had been placed in the late nineteenth century after house building disturbed the abbey remains.

Right: This impression of the seal of Keynsham's Hospice of St John the Baptist is the only real evidence we have for the existence of this late medieval establishment. The present whereabouts of the seal is unknown.

Left: Tradition states that these two stone figures – one fat, one thin – came from above the entrance to the hospice. In the nineteenth century, they supported a bay window in a house opposite the west end of the parish church and now form part of a garden rockery and are fondly known as Gog and Magog.

This interior view of Keynsham Church shows the nave aisle leading to the chancel. The candelabra were made in a local brass mill and presented to the church by Mrs Ann Tilly in 1717 and 1721.

Keynsham Parish Church dates from 1292 at the latest. The south aisle was constructed in the thirteenth century and the north aisle in the fourteenth. The western tower was built in the seventeenth century after the original north-east tower was struck by lightening. Notice the ornate lamp post, which was recently seriously damaged by a car.

Above: Situated at the east end of the south aisle of the church is a beautiful fifteenth-century timber screen. The organ loft is above and the central doorway leads to the present choir vestry.

Opposite: On the south wall of the chancel of the church is a large, elaborate memorial to Sir Thomas Bridges, who died in 1661, aged twenty years, within two months of being knighted. The Bridges family bought the remains of Keynsham Abbey after its dissolution and were patrons of the parish church.

This interesting relic of the Victorian era was used to accommodate a gentleman's top hat during the church service. The hoop swivelled backwards and forwards under the nave-side seat of the third pew on the left from the front. Unfortunately, it disappeared during repairs to the church in 1998.

The ceiling of the south aisle is decorated with painted wooden bosses, two of which are illustrated here. One represents the 'green man' with foliage sprouting from his mouth, but it is uncertain what the other depicts.

In 1902, Keynsham had four wall letter boxes sited in Bath Hill, Bristol Road, the Gasworks and Chewton Keynsham. The first three were cleared four times a day. This shows a George Rex example in Station Road. One of the Victorian ones is in Bath Postal Museum.

This familiar red telephone box stood at the top of Chewton Hill, near its junction with Wellsway, until June 2003, when it suddenly disappeared! Although showing signs of neglect, it was treasured by local people.

One rarely looks beneath one's feet, but street furniture such as this iron grating in Steel Mills can be interesting historical items. This grating dates from between 1894 and 1933, when the area was in Keynsham Rural District, although Keynsham had its own parish council..

In Bristol Road, one can find several very old manhole covers. This one, manufactured by Bush & Wilton of Bitton, dates from between 1933 and 1936, when Keynsham was within the Bathavon Rural District of Somerset County.

Situated near the previous one, this manhole cover was laid before 1974 when Keynsham, after hundreds of years in ancient Somerset, was politically (and needlessly) moved into a new county called Avon.

This road sign at the junction of Manor Road with Wellsway is another reminder of happier days when Keynsham was part of Somerset.

Stanton & Stavely made this sewer cover according to British Standard 497 as can be seen by the Kitemark. This quality standard was introduced in 1903 for tramway rails and manhole covers. Later, it encompassed many types of manufactured goods and is in use still.

Left: Chandos Lodge, the old hunting lodge of the Bridges family, was recently refurbished. These are some of the pre-Victorian rainwater guttering fitments which were replaced.

Opposite below: This, the Dapifers's House, is one of Keynsham's oldest surviving houses. A dapifer was a person who brought meat to the table or a royal steward. The house is situated in Dapps Hill, just above the River Chew.

Above: Keynsham people had their own telephone numbers by 1927. There was a public telephone call office at 33 Rock Road between 1931 and 1935. The telephone exchange building is still extant on the corner between Ladoc and Culvers Roads. The Valley Water Colour Mill was Keynsham 3 and the Co-op in the High Street was Keynsham 4. Who was Keynsham 1? Alas, the Keynsham telephone exchange no longer exists and we all have Bristol numbers now.

Not far from the Dapifer's House, at the top of a flight of stone steps, is this ancient stone stile. It is unusual in having a special gap through which animals, such as dogs, may pass.

For many, many years, this charming little gazebo has been an attractive feature in the garden of Ellsbridge House. Art classes often sat on the lawn to draw and paint it. The house dates from the mid-nineteenth century, but was built onto a much older farmhouse and is now owned by the Bath and North-East Somerset Council, who demolished the gazebo in June 2003.

INVITATION

....

ARE INVITED TO ATTEND THE LAUNCH OF THE

KEYNSHAM & NORTH WANSDYKE HERITAGE TRUST

ON FRIDAY 10th APRIL 1987 at 7.30 p.m.
AT ST. JOHNS PARISH CHURCH HALL, KEYNSHAM
GUEST SPEAKERS:-
COUNC. LES SELL, CHAIRMAN OF LEISURE & AMENITIES COMMITTEE
KENNETH HUDSON, NATIONAL AUTHORITY ON MUSEUMS

EXHIBITION - MUSIC BY THE "AMMONITES"
SLIDES - HISTORIC FILM - OTHER ENTERTAINMENT
REFRESHMENTS

RSVP TO KEYNSHAM PUBLIC LIBRARY BY 21 MARCH 1987

Keynsham has a very rich and important heritage, which has been systematically destroyed by successive planners. In April 1987, caring local people formed a heritage trust to try to raise funds for a museum in which to house the valuable Roman and medieval artefacts rescued from destruction.

A local architect, Julian Hannan, designed this imaginative plan for the museum. It was to have display areas, school and research rooms, a lecture theatre and a café, with full facilities for the disabled. Sadly, the necessary funding for the building was unavailable, although the Friends of the Musem group organised various fund-raising events.

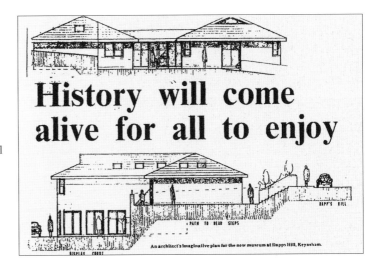

History will come alive for all to enjoy

An architect's imaginative plan for the new museum at Dapps Hill, Keynsham.

The council earmarked a piece of land at the end of Temple Street for the buildings. Formerly, a large house, the Pines, and a chapel occupied the site, but local residents opposed the scheme. This picture shows the site in 1993.

Over the years, the trustees of the Keynsham Heritage Trust have organised a series of activities for children during school holidays. These trustees – Eric Linfield, Barbara Lowe, Margaret Whitehead and Tony Brown – entered into the spirit of Roman Keynsham.

An exhibition to celebrate 2000 years of a North Somerset town:

May 8th to May 13th 2000

Left: This is the cover of a leaflet produced to advertise a very large exhibition of Keynsham's heritage in May 2000, which was organised jointly by the Folk House Archaeological Society, the Keynsham Heritage Trust and the Keynsham and Saltford Local History Society. Roman and medieval artefacts were displayed in the parish church with historical documents and information in the parish hall.

Below: At the end of June 2003, members of the above societies participated in Channel 4's *Time Team Big Dig* by providing on-site excavation experience for seventeen local applicants. The weekend was a huge success, the weather gorgeous and archaeological 'finds' prolific – refreshments were freely provided by Cadbury's. Here are Sue Catford, Elaine Smith, Barbara Lowe (director), Andrew Parry and Steve Shepherd happily at work.

three

Floods

Keynsham's most devastating floods occurred on the night of 10 July 1968. Rain had fallen for day after day until all the ground and local hills were saturated. The Rivers Avon and Chew were overflowing when a huge tidal wave swept down the Chew, sweeping away or severely damaging ancient stone bridges in its path. Keynsham was officially declared a disaster area and the Duke of Edinburgh visited here the next day. The thirteenth-century stone bridge, whose central point marked the division between Somersetshire and Gloucestershire, was damaged beyond repair as can be seen here.

It would appear that since Keynsham's mills ceased to operate, the area has been subject to regular flooding. At 1.45 p.m. on 3 June 1925, this photograph was taken of the River Avon from Fry's factory site. On the extreme right is the old county bridge and the distant building is the White Hart Inn, which dates from at least 1678, when its occupant was Valentine Palmer.

Another serious flood occurred in 1928. This photograph, taken from near Fry's power house, shows the old bridge and the inn in deeper water than the previous one. The cone of Avon Brass Mill's furnace can be seen beyond the bridge.

Here, on 30 November 1929, we are looking across the (once more) flooded Avon, this time from the Willsbridge Road towards Fry's Factory, which almost stands on an island.

The same floods affected the River Chew and, similarly, the residents of the Colour Mill appear isolated as they gaze towards Avon Mill Lane. The house in the background was demolished in the 1960s.

The winter of 1946/47 was very harsh. High rainfall and melting snow in March created this watery scene. On the right, the old county bridge appears wet but passable. At the midpoint of the bridge is the huge stone fondly known as the 'Abbot's Chair', placed there to mark the boundary between Somerset and Gloucestershire.

Paddling was such a temptation for the children returning from school, but the forlorn lad in the foreground was wearing only shoes and dared not join his booted friends on the Bitton Road in March 1947.

The dreadful floods of 10 July 1968 left a trail of devastation. The parapet of the Town Bridge at the bottom of Bath Hill was swept away, and although traffic on 11 July was able to pass over at first, a hole suddenly appeared in the road during the morning and traffic had to be banned from passing that way. All vehicles had to use the bypass to get from one side of the town to the other.

The next bridge up the River Chew was this one at Crox Bottom or Dapps Hill. The houses nearby were badly flooded and one resident had to be rescued from an upstairs window by boat. The parapet was swept away but the bridge remained in use.

Sadly, lives were lost when two cars were swept from Town Bridge into the flooded River Chew on 10 July 1968. At dawn, a helicopter managed to rescue one passenger who was clinging to a tree.

Some people helped to recover the vehicles as the waters receded on 11 July. Others watched operations in silence as the extent of devastation became apparent.

Although the River Avon was re-routed after 1968 and a new bridge built on a different alignment, extensive flooding occurred on 21 January 1995. Keynsham Lock became almost submerged.

On the same day, Keynsham Hams were flooded and grazing sheep had to be rescued and moved to higher ground nearer the factory. The River Avon is in the foreground.

This award-winning bandstand of the 1960s stood near the Colour Mill weir in Keynsham Park. Although almost submerged by the 1968 floods, it survived for some years before being destroyed. Only the base remains today.

A useful shop selling refreshments formed the rear of the bandstand unit and toilets were next door. These were badly damaged and never re-opened.

four

Transport

A new bus service was introduced by Bristol Tramways & Carriage Co. Ltd on 5 February 1906 to link Keynsham to the villages of Brislington and Saltford. Here, a Thornycroft bus is seen outside the Lamb and Lark Hotel in Keynsham High Street, soon after the service started. (M.J. Tozer Collection)

This smart hansom cab was Keynsham's 'taxi' in the years before the First World War. The cabman was known as 'Spanky Fisher'. The hansom cab, so popular in London and other large cities during Victorian times, was invented by Joseph Hansom in the 1830s.

At the same time, private cars also started to appear on the streets of Keynsham. This three-wheeler dates from 1914. Such cars were classified as motorcycles and teenagers as young as fourteen were permitted to drive them on public roads. (M.J. Tozer Collection).

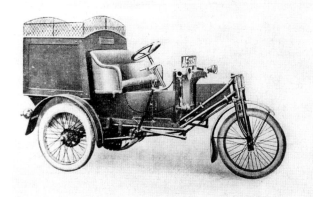

The "AVON"

LIGHT

Delivery Van.

Telegraphic Address: "Avon Motor," Saltford, Bristol.
Telephone No. 21Y. Keynsham.

The AVON MOTOR
MANUFACTURING Co.,
KEYNSHAM, BRISTOL.

Some three-wheelers were constructed as commercial vehicles. This light delivery van, with a top speed of 20mph, was built in 1910 by Avon Manufacturing Co. of Bath Road, Keynsham. The proprietor of the business was George Henshaw.

The migration of the large cocoa and chocolate manufactory of J.S. Fry & Sons Ltd from Bristol to Keynsham in the 1920s brought with it a great variety of transport, although this horse-drawn van is from an earlier decade.

Fry's continued to use horse-drawn transport in the 1920s, as indicated by the signage on this dray. Somerdale was the name chosen in 1924 for the new factory site in Keynsham, following a nationwide competition.

Much of the material used to build the Somerdale factory came by river from Bristol in barges such as this one, owned by F.A. Ashmead & Son. A special riverside jetty for such transport was constructed at Somerdale in 1921.

A chauffeur-driven car is seen at Fry's Somerdale factory in the 1920s. This form of transport would have been in great demand at that time to convey senior managers of the company between the Bristol and Keynsham factories.

These Albion delivery vans with electric lighting, pneumatic tyres and enclosed cabs, were the last word in commercial vehicles when introduced into Fry's transport fleet in the late 1920s. The vans were built by the Albion Motor Car Co. Ltd of Scotstoun, Glasgow.

The company's sales representatives, known then as commercial travellers, pose with their Morris vans near the Fry's factory in this photograph from the early 1930s. In the background is the steel frame of one of the factory buildings still under construction.

Bulk supplies of raw materials, such as cocoa beans and sugar, were delivered to Somerdale by rail via a siding from the main Bristol to London line at Keynsham Station. Here the cutting for the siding, opened in 1924, is being constructed. The overbridge at Keynsham Station is seen in the left background.

Railway vans were shunted from Keynsham Station by main-line locomotives and had to cross the Willsbridge Road by an ungated level crossing. In later years, diesel locomotives of the type seen here did the work. The siding remained in use until September 1978.

As soon as the railway vans had been transferred from the main line, they were moved around the factory site by Fry's own Sentinel locomotive. This view dates from August 1928.

Fry's also used the national rail network extensively for publicity with their own exhibition train. In this 1932 photograph, the show train is ready with stepladders in place to receive visitors.

The company's products also took to the air. Here, factory workers load boxes, watched by an appreciative crowd of colleagues. The air service started on 13 September 1932, with the small Puss-moth aircraft involved taking off from the company's sports field.

Despite the factory development, Keynsham's High Street still kept its tranquil unhurried look, as shown in this view from the mid-1920s. One car, one lorry and one bicycle are the only examples of wheeled transport apart from perambulators, but there is now a garage to cater for motorists' needs.

In this view, the High Street is seen from the top end of Bristol Road, with Station Road leading to Fry's factory off to the left. It is a mid-afternoon scene from about 1930, with St John's Church clock showing 2.55 p.m. There is just one car on the move and two others parked, so there is no need for yellow lines or traffic wardens. (M.J. Tozer Collection)

The garage in Keynsham's High Street continued in business for several decades and was known as St Keyna Motor Works from about 1926. Pedestrians were inconvenienced when the petrol pump arms had to be swung across the pavement. Here, in a scene reminiscent of the 1940s, a Ford Anglia passes a Standard 8 which has lost a spare wheel.

Keynsham Station here shows the substantial overbridge for pedestrians, which was removed in 1970 and re-erected at a preserved steam railway in Devon. The central part of the bridge was blackened by smoke from the steam locomotives.

A train stands at Keynsham Station towards the end of the steam era. All steam locomotives were withdrawn from regular main-line work by 1968. Keynsham was also to lose its Victorian station buildings. These were demolished in 1970, although a limited number of trains still stop here, more than thirty years later.

Before the downsizing of Keynsham Station, Fry's were already making more use of road transport to move their materials around the country. This Foden tanker for bulk liquids was new in May 1958.

Eighty years separate this and the next view of heavy horses at work in Keynsham. This one dates from around 1922.

This second view shows a twenty-first-century innovation by the local council to collect household waste for recycling.

five

Wartime

Queen Mary visited Fry's chocolate factory on 19 January 1940. In this unusual photograph of a member of the royal family, the Queen is seen sampling one of the freshly made chocolates. Queen Mary was then a widow, her husband King George V having died on 20 January 1936.

War was declared against Germany on 3 September 1939 and thousands of men and women were called up for military service. On 2 November 1939, '1' Troop 7/2nd Somerset Light Infantry Regiment RA visited Fry's factory. In the background is Avonfield House, the head office of the firm. This building was demolished early in 2003.

Every person in the country was issued with a gas mask in case the Germans resorted to gas warfare. Some of these ungainly and uncomfortable masks are seen on the table in the foreground as Fry's workers received their own. Everyone had to carry their mask at all times and schoolchildren had regular classroom drills in how to put them on and wear them.

The extensive factory grounds at Fry's were used for training local defence units. Factories, shops, offices and even senior schools formed their own emergency teams for such contingencies as fire fighting (with stirrup pumps), first aid and general air-raid precautions. This decontamination squad is receiving instruction given by a lady on 3 November 1939.

On her morale-boosting visit to the factory in January 1940, Cecil Fry (chairman of the directors) watches as a worker presents Queen Mary with a huge, satin-topped box of special chocolates.

'Dig for Victory' was a favourite slogan in the spring of 1940. People were urged to dig up their own gardens, rent allotments and to grow as many food crops as possible in order to supplement rationed foodstuffs. Fry's took the lead locally by ploughing and planting sports fields.

Fry's called this their kitchen garden. Vegetables were grown for use in the works canteen. The houses in Chandos Road and Keynsham Parish Church are in the background.

Another garden on the north side of the factory produced spinach, beet, peas and broad beans.

In furtherance of the war effort, sheep were reared on the former playing fields. The nets are in a sorry state.

The cart bears the name 'Clothier of [something] Hill Farm'. Could this have been Pen Hill Farm, Queen Charlton? The people working here were involved in making silage on 12 June 1941. Were you one of the youngsters helping or watching?

We are unsure of the identity of this military group whose photograph was taken between 1940 and 1945. It may be the local Territorial Army. Were you there?

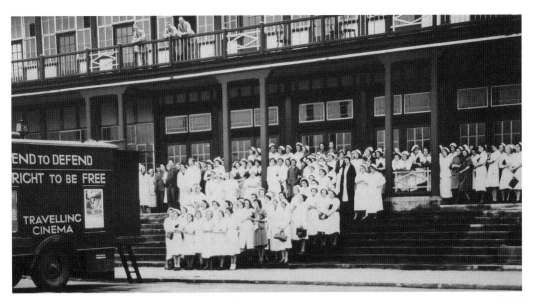

During the war, everything possible was done to maintain the morale of workers everywhere. Travelling cinemas enabled workers to watch entertaining films in their lunch breaks. This was promoting a War Savings week.

No.2 Company of the 7th Battalion Somerset Local Defence Volunteers became the Home Guard in August 1940. Their HQ was in the old police station on Bath Hill and the call-out code word was Cromwell. Here, members have gathered together for a group photograph. Rex Harris is seated second from the right in the front row. Can you name anyone else?

The girls in this photograph have put up bunting and Union Jacks to celebrate Victory in Europe (VE) Day on 7 May 1945.

During the war, sweets and chocolates were severely rationed, so on VE Day this young lady displays a tray of Fry's Chocolate Cream Bars. Sweet rationing did not end until 24 April 1949, and then only temporarily because shops were besieged and soon sold their stock. For this reason, rationing was resumed on 14 August that year.

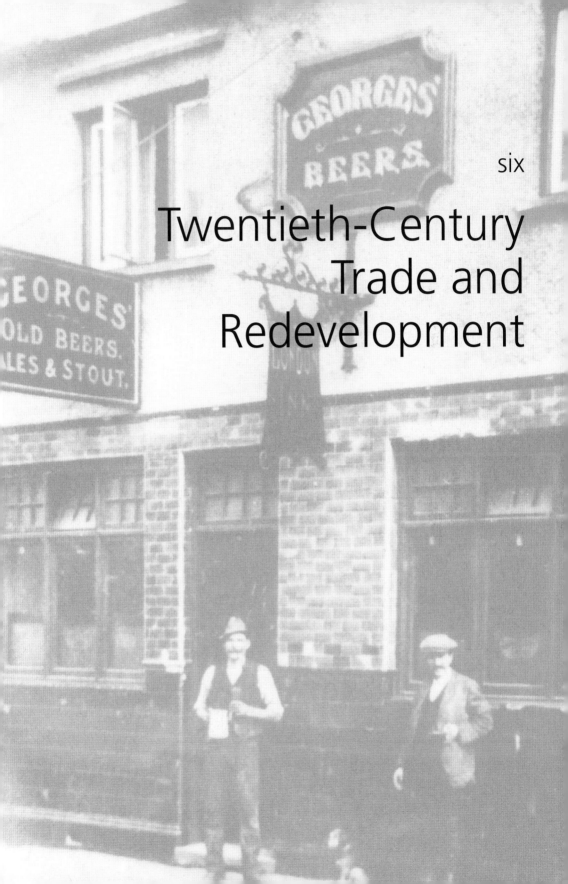

six

Twentieth-Century Trade and Redevelopment

Avonfields House, once the head office of Fry's, was built in the 1930s and was the height of elegance. Cecil Fry unveiled a plaque in March 1932 to mark the move from Bristol. In 1936, Fry's became part of Cadbury's, but not until 1968 did Fry's and Cadbury's become the Cadbury Group. Avonfield's House was leased to various organisations in the 1980s. In 2002, it became disused and was gradually emptied of all contents until it was completely demolished in 2003. This picture was taken on 4 July 2002.

Keynsham established its own gas company in 1857. The works were built by Atkins & Son at the bottom of Dapps Hill and came into operation on 16 January 1858. In 1928, the works were sold to the Bristol Gas Company. This early twentieth-century picture shows the tops of the two gasometers and the chimney behind the manager's house.

A new retort house, new purifiers and condensers were installed in 1925, and the former survived as offices until 2001 when work began on redevelopment of the site for housing. The bases of the two gasometers were exposed, this picture showing the larger one on 5 September 2001.

Willoughby's Family Grocers and Provision Merchants had a shop in Temple Street. This picture shows a window of the shop in 1890, with Charles Willoughby, the proprieter, standing on the left. Notice the provisions and prices.

Above: Frederick John Frankham ran this supply stores and grocery at Park View, at the bottom of Wellsway, from about 1927 until 1934. To the left of the picture is the fountain which was built to commemorate Queen Victoria's Golden Jubilee and nearby is an old gas street lamp.

Left: This vehicle, a tri-mobile (classed as a motorcycle), was produced by the Avon Motor Manufacturing Co. of Bath Road, Keynsham. Fourteen-year-old A.E. Cannock was able to take his aunt, Miss E. Cox, for a drive in 1911.

Cannock's garage and workshop, seen in 1961, with Shell petrol pumps in the forecourt. This business was started in 1919 at the bottom of Bristol Hill, opposite St Ladoc Road.

Here, we see Cannock's car showroom and offices in 1961. The office was in Homeleigh Cottage, seen behind the petrol pumps. This was formerly two cottages and although the deeds date back to 1748, the properties were older. When turnpiking raised the road, the ground floors of these cottages were left below the new level.

Yet more of Keynsham's heritage was wantonly destroyed when Homeleigh was demolished in April-May 2003. Both Edward and David Cannock were born in the old house. The site still remains undeveloped.

In the 1920s and 1930s, businessmen and tradesmen took their families on annual outings to places like Cheddar or Weston-super-Mare. This open-topped coach has already been loaded with the women and children, whilst the wage-earners pose stiffly for this photograph before setting off in 1924.

Right: This was the London Inn, Temple Street, just before the Second World War. Three-quarters of the houses in Temple Street were recklessly demolished in 1960s and 1970s. Pleas were made between 1967 and 1973 for the conservation of this old inn, but all failed and it was destroyed with everything else.

Below: Messrs Bailey and Maddicks stand outside their motor engineering business in Keynsham High Street in 1930. Originally, there were two cottages on this site and these were rebuilt in 1904 as the Picture House. This closed in 1918 and Walter Beak began the motor business here in 1919, succeeded by Henry Jaques who ran it until 1926.

The junction of the High Street with Bath Hill and Temple Street in September 1979 shows shops that have changed hands several times since then. Rawlings, formerly a well-known cycle stockist, opened a hobby and model kit store at the top of the hill and Mervyn Holmes' Garden Shop is to its left. Both these families were 'old Keynsham'. Left again was Ogborn's Newsagent and Stationers, another long-standing local business. Everyone was sad when they closed.

This serene picture shows Fry's Somerdale factory from Keynsham Hams in March 1934. Stone boundary walls, several hundred years old, are still extant here, although beginning to crumble. The Hams had never been ploughed, but had provided rich pasture land for fattening cattle.

When Fry's came to Keynsham in 1921-22, a working farm existed on part of the site. It was a large, seemingly ancient farm with extensive barns and stables. The last known occupants were Albert Clothier and Rhoda, his wife, who lived to be ninety-nine years old. Was the farm named Chandos Farm? In order to provide houses for workers, Fry's demolished the farm and constructed new homes served by the newly made Chandos Road.

This little lodge house was built just inside Fry's main gates in 1926 to house Roman artefacts from the small villa discovered during factory construction. The firm's weighbridge may be seen in the foreground. The building was demolished in 1990.

Tours of the chocolate factory in Somerdale Garden City were in great demand. Here, forty-eight visitor guides are assembled outside the little lodge, ready to conduct visitors around the site on 25 June 1930.

Left: Fry's installed all the latest machinery for the production of their Milk and Belgrave Chocolates. Here, a cocoa press is making cocoa cakes in October 1930.

Opposite: Neatly dressed workers walk or cycle down the tree-lined drive on their way home after their shift in 1930. Many workers lived in Keynsham, whilst others commuted by train to Bristol or Bath. The train service was excellent in those days.

This advertisement was produced in 1978, on the 250th anniversary of the company. The world-famous Five Boy advertisement was produced under the aegis of Conrad P. Fry and gave a far-reaching impetus to sales. It was first used in 1886 but became a household name from 1902. Five Boys chocolate was withdrawn from sale in 1970. The model for the photograph was Lindsay Paulton.

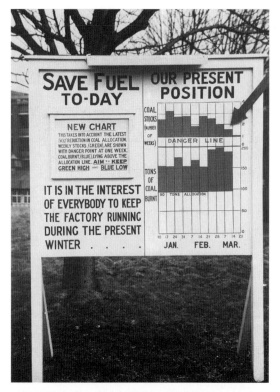

The winter of 1947 was very harsh and there was a great shortage of coal. Everyone was urged to save fuel and this chart was erected outside Fry's factory to inform workers of the current position in March 1947.

Fry's slogan was 'Happiness in Industry' and the firm always felt a certain responsibility for the spiritual, mental and physical welfare of their employees. This picture shows three young workers relaxing amongst the daffodils during their lunch break in 1952.

CUSTOMER CARD

Church Bakery

16, High Street, Keynsham, Bristol

IN THE EVENT OF A
BREAD STRIKE THIS CARD
GUARANTEES YOUR BREAD

In 1978, there was national bread strike – some people travelled miles to find a baker with bread for sale. This Keynsham bakery issued cards to its regular customers on 8 November 1978, so that they would be assured of obtaining their usual order.

We are unsure when this building became an inn or why its name relates to hunting dogs – Talbot hounds. In 1841, the building was owned by Samuel Skuse, who ran the Lamb and Lark, and the landlord in 1873 was George Anstey. This photograph was taken in 1978 when it was a Courage house. It is now a 'steak and ale' pub.

The Ivy Lodge Hotel once stood on this site, but a large Esso service station was built here in 1960s. Unfortunately, in August 1983, it was demolished and a differently designed service station built in its place.

The Kasbah in Temple Street was an Aladdin's cave full of second-hand domestic articles. Everything from prams and toys to antique furniture could be found there. The building itself was from the sixteenth century and a listed building, but that did not stop a developer from destroying it (without planning permission) in 1995. The central building was a garage repair shop and, to the right, Tina's hairdressing shop.

The Avon Drug Stores was another shop in Temple Street which was closed down and the building redesigned. It is now the Bread Basket.

To the right of the Avon Drug Stores was the Roberts Wine Shop and the Trustee Savings Bank. The former building is now Gamescene and the latter is part of Iceland.

Keynsham's old post office occupied this building (1875 to 1926), which is next door to the Baptist chapel in the High Street. The property was sold to A.E. Mills in 1926. The well-known chemists, Mills & Mills, occupied the premises and continued to do so until the 1970s. Later, the building was divided into two shops and there has been a succession of small businesses since.

Milward Lodge at the bottom of St Ladoc Road was once a farm and, in the 1920s, an abattoir. Stories are told of how parts of the dead animals blocked the drains leading under the road, through Hawkeswell Field to the river. The stones topping the front wall were brought from the Preseli Mountains.

Milward Lodge and its site have recently been redeveloped. During the work, the stream running down the side of the house, alongside St Ladoc Road, was uncovered. This stream appears to rise somewhere around Broadlands, cross under Ladoc Road and continue under Bristol Road, eventually reaching the River Avon.

seven

People and Events

The Rivers Chew and Avon have always played a major role in the lives of Keynsham people, both for transport and leisure. The first local regatta was held in 1849 on the River Avon at Saltford, a few miles upriver. This interesting picture shows crowds of spectators at the regatta of 1910.

There were various clubs and societies connected with Fry's which contributed to the greater happiness and well-being of the employees. On 23 May 1933, four new tennis courts were completed and were immediately put into good use by the girls.

How better to relax after a strenuous game of tennis than to see-saw and pose for this happy picture in 1933.

Opposite below: Wellsway was formerly called Burnett Lane and this was widened in 1923. The workmen were, from left to right, back row: Newman, Trengrove, Hatcher, Greenland, Ollis, Newman, Williams, Carter, Macey. Front row: J. Bees, Vailes, Lowman, Williams (Ratler), Glover, Alward, F. Collins.

Above: Bowls was a favourite sport for the male workers and a new bowling green was prepared for them in June 1933. The site was at the end of Chandos Road.

Left: Mr J.G. Harvey, seen here on 10 May 1938, aged ninety, was England's oldest working newsagent at that time. He started the business in 1889 from an ancient cottage in Station Road, Keynsham, in which he had lived since 1877.

Right: Mr Ted Warren, seen here in 1950, owned and farmed Uplands Farm on the Wellsway from after the Second World War until his death.

Below: The Festival of Britain Exhibition was held in London in 1951 to mark the centenary of the Great Exhibition held at the Crystal Palace in 1851. Keynsham and Saltford Arts Club staged their own festival exhibition at the Fear Institute, Mary Fairclough being the prime mover. Local industries and societies were invited to contribute displays. This one was by Gould, Thomas & Co., dry-salters of Albert Road.

This fascinating display of old costumes, lace and needlecraft puts our modern-day 'boughten' shop wear to shame. The skills, patience and craftsmanship of our parents and grandparents seem to be dying out.

The award-winning avant garde bandstand, built on the site of Downe or the Colour Mill in the 1960s, was badly damaged in the 1968 floods and eventually dismantled. The bandstand was a favourite gathering site on sunny afternoons in the park. Concerts were held on summer weekends and the little refreshments shop was well used.

A 'Goodbye to Somerset' exhibition was staged in 1974 in Keynsham Parish Hall. As was the case in 1951, local industries and societies mounted displays. This one illustrates products from the Keynsham Brass Battery Mill (Avon Mill), together with pictures relating to its history and the brass-making process.

Left: Fry's set up this special display showing examples of emergency chocolate ration packs issued to servicemen during the war. Some very elegant be-ribboned chocolate boxes are seen on the shelves.

Below: Here are four stalwart members of the Keynsham Fireside Men's Fellowship, enjoying their annual dinner in the 1970s. From left to right: Jim Allen, Councillor Percy Baker, Dick Coates and Norman Holland. The Fellowship was founded in 1937 and holds weekly meetings from October through to March.

Right: 'Victorian ladies', accompanied by 'Isambard K. Brunel', greet a rather surprised train driver at Keynsham Station on 31 August 1990. The ladies (Barbara Lowe and Margaret Whitehead) presented red carnations to the driver and alighting passengers from the early commuter trains to mark the 150th anniversary of the opening of Keynsham Station.

Below: A happy ENSA group entertains onlookers outside Fry Club during celebrations to commemorate the 50th anniversary of VE (Victory in Europe) Day on 7 May 1995.

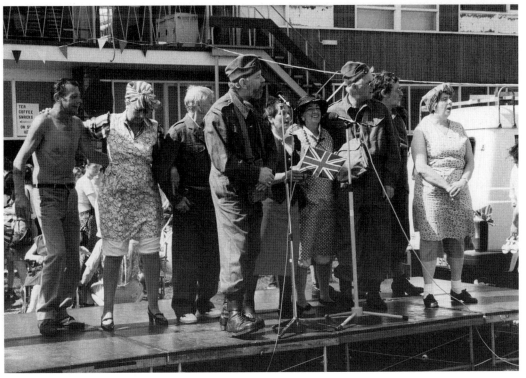

Wansdyke District Council succeeded the Keynsham Urban District Council in 1974 and was itself superceded by Bath and North-East Somerset in 1996. Keynsham Town Hall, with its elegant council chamber, was purpose-built in the 1960s.

The Keynsham Heritage Trust staged an exhibition relating to the history of Keynsham in 1998. This was a week-long display and was held in the Victoria Methodist Church.

The Keynsham Heritage 2000 Exhibition was held in St John's Church and in the parish hall from 8 to 13 May. One of the displays was this portion of Roman pavement from Keynsham's large villa under the cemetery.

This interesting Holy Water stoup, carved from one solid block of stone, was also exhibited at this exhibition. It came from the ruins of Keynsham Abbey disturbed by house building between 1865 and 1885 and since then has been used to decorate a folly arch.

A flower festival was held in Keynsham Church in June 2001. This attractive display was arranged by members of St Michael's Church, Burnett.

Left: Members of the Bridges Society, which raises money to help restore parts of the fabric of the church, composed this delightful arrangement in the font given by Harry Bridges in 1725.

Below: The Keynsham Millenium Mosaic project was funded by Keynsham Town Council, supported by B & NES Keynsham Town Centre Management and directed by the B & NES Museums Education Service. The chairman of the Keynsham Town Council, Peter Oakey, launched the Mosaic Trail on 20 August 2002. Margaret Whitehead led the first trail.

The mosaics are all on display in flower beds in the town centre. This Fry/Cadbury mosaic was worked by members of the St John's Church Youth Group.

Members of the Keynsham Community Association made this mosaic which depicts the workhouse (now Keynsham Hospital) and the much loved and lamented Lamb and Lark Hotel.

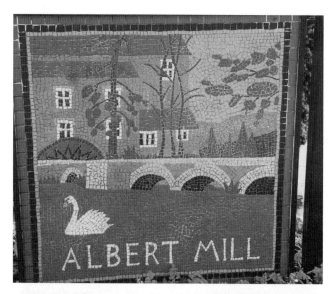

Facets of Keynsham's history were taken as themes for the mosaics, each group choosing its own theme. The Albert Mill was worked by members of Age Concern and their families.

The Abbot of Keynsham was granted a charter in 1303 for a weekly market and an annual fair. Reaffirmed in 1575, both market and fair thrived for another 200 years. The weekly Thursday market continued to be held until 1889. Then, from 1923 to 1975, a weekly cattle and produce market was held at the site upon which Homeavon flats now stand. This picture shows the market in 1933.

An attempt to restore Keynsham's weekly market was made in November 2002. It was held on Fridays on the town centre forecourt but was discontinued in September 2003.

Local residents expected the market to sell local farm produce, but the stalls sell miscellaneous goods and very little local produce.

An unusual sight outside the Fear Institute was this helter-skelter, set up for Keynsham's annual Victorian evening on 29 November 2002.

A Royal Golden Jubilee Exhibition was organised by members of the Keynsham and Saltford Local History Society in November 2002. This shows one corner of the display in the Fear Institute, with chairman Sue Trude in charge.

Keynsham's annual spring flower show was held in the Fear Institute on April 2003. Some of the exhibits are on display in this picture, and Gordon Pett is seen engrossed in the daffodils. Behind him are Harold Rees (show manager), Geoff Saunders (who recently retired as chairman after many years) and Ann Martin (committee member).

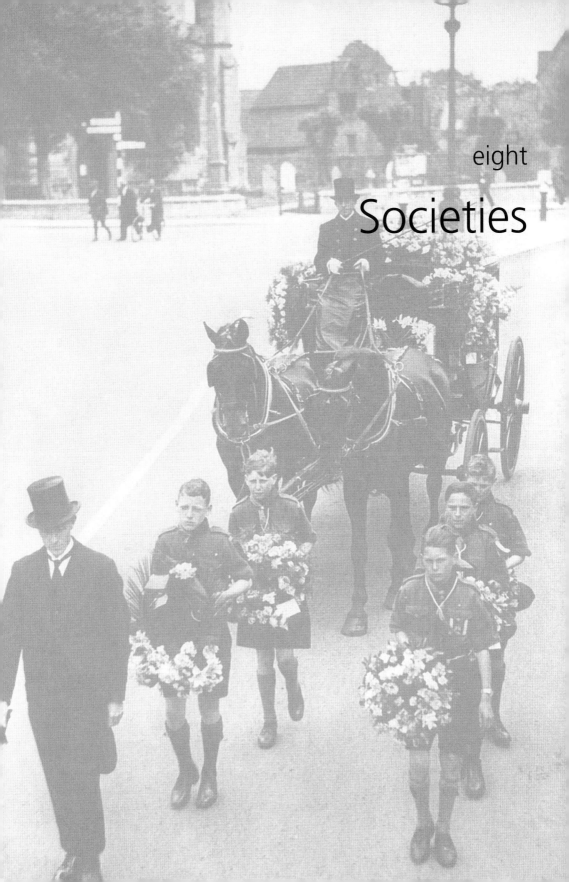

eight

Societies

Junior members of the Keynsham Shotokai Karate Club demonstrate their skills at a school fête in June 2002. The group includes, from left to right, front row: Sarah Gibbs, Gemma and Rachel Emes (sisters). The instructor with her back to the camera is Kate Jones.

Members of the Keynsham Division of the St John Ambulance Brigade assemble for their first annual inspection at their Rock Road headquarters, May 1985. The group includes divisional surgeon Dr Christopher Bailey (seventh from the left, second row). He was one of the town's GPs for many years.

This commemorates the presentation and dedication of the ambulance for use by the Keynsham Division, St John Ambulance Brigade. Those present at the ceremony outside St John the Baptist Church, Keynsham, on 2 December 1984 include Reverend Richard Frith (rector of Keynsham) and divisional superintendent Barbara Hill (fourth from the left).

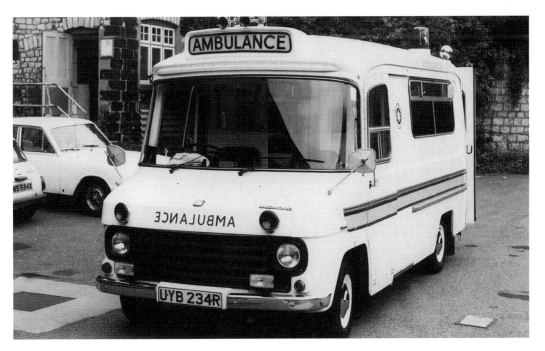

The Bedford ambulance was acquired second hand from the Somerset County Ambulance Service and was kept temporarily at the Keynsham Paper Mills, near Avon Mill Lane, while the Keynsham Division sought a new, permanent headquarters.

The former Salvation Army hut in Rock Road became available during 1984, and St John Ambulance moved in, initially as tenants, but taking over as owners from 1985. Later this old building was replaced by a modern prefabricated structure, with a gated yard at the rear to provide space for two ambulances. Here, Barbara Hill assists with spring cleaning!

The Keynsham and Saltford Local History Society organises an annual coach trip for members and friends. Here, a guide is explaining points of interest outside Malmesbury Abbey on 18 June 1994. Facing us, from left to right, we see: Joan Butler, -?-, Dennis Hill, Margaret Shore, Tony Brown, Michael Fitter, Betty Millard, Bunty Dunford, Elizabeth White, John Dunford.

In 1997, the society visited Shaftesbury on a very hot day. One member of the group (Mary Mitchell) was sensible enough to bring a sunshade and Hilary Smedley (right) wore an outsize hat. The tall figure on the left is Dennis Hill.

John and Bunty Dunford, with Sheila and Eric Linfield, walk around the gardens at Tintinhull House in 1993. This was a joint visit by the Folk House Archaeological Society and the Keynsham and Saltford Local History Society.

Members of these two societies maintain the Abbey ruins at Keynsham, tending the medieval herb gardens there. This group of workers are seen resting from their labours on 14 May 2003. From left to right: Doug Sprague, Merle Wade, Muriel Sprague, Mary Lanning, Ann Starr, Robin Stiles, Michael Starr, Margaret Whitehead.

St John's Amateur Dramatic Society, Keynsham, produced *The Holly and the Ivy* in March 1965, with, from left to right, Jim Allen, Mary Green, Richard Allen and Maude Deere. The society originates from 1949, when the Guild of St Hilda co-opted some men to assist in the staging of one-act plays.

Actors in the production of *Charley's Aunt* in November 1970 included, from left to right, Jane Quartly, Chris Sullivan, Alan Chives and Naomi Hunter. Prior to 1960, plays were rehearsed in the Old School Room, Station Road, Keynsham. Scenery was stored there and transported by handcart to the Fear Institute in Keynsham High Street, where it had to be hurriedly erected and prepared before the dress rehearsal.

After the demolition of the Old School Room to make way for the Keynsham bypass in 1963, St John the Baptist Church Hall became the venue for productions. The society changed its name to St John's Drama Group in 1990s. This scene is from the November 2001 production of *Pools Paradise*.

Above: The November 2002 production of *My Friend Miss Flint* included, from left to right, John Palser, Juliet Chastney, Peter Irwin (group chairman) and Gill Stirling. The group continues to perform one or two plays a year in the church hall.

Opposite: This sad picture shows the cortège of Ronald Arthur Sparey, aged just sixteen years, being led by the other five members of his scout patrol on its way to Keynsham Cemetery, where he was buried on 20 August 1929. He had been playing cricket and went for a swim in the River Chew to cool off. The official cause of death was pneumonia, but his family believed it was caused by Weil's disease, which is carried by rats.

Above: Lord Strachey is seen here planting a tree at the Keynsham Scouts' headquarters in 1928, assisted by R.J.C. Smith (Bob), leader of Peewit Patrol. Others present were, to the left of Bob: Alan Llea, Davis, Dennis Healey, Peewits Newman, John Reynolds. Right of Bob were: Les White, Cub Watts, Fred Sweet. Behind him was Ted Taylor and behind Strachey were Viv Turner, Reg Turner, Cub Monty Veale, Revd Warren, Storme Hale SM, John Downton ASM.

Opposite above: This shows the encampment at Corston for the Scouts annual jamboree of 1932. Hundreds of tents were set up on land owned by Mr Collins.

Opposite below: Keynsham Scouts – from left to right: Jack Veales, -?-, Gordon Reed, -?-, Alan Lea, Bob Webb, John Downton ASM – are gathered around their 'modern' gramophone at the Jamboree.

Above: Scouts were encouraged to participate in all kinds of activities. Here, a group inspects the results of their archery practice.

Opposite above: Another group of Keynsham Scouts at the 1932 West Country jamboree. Can anyone supply names?

Opposite below: This group of Scouts from the 1st Keynsham and Somerdale troop pose for a photograph at Bridgwater in 1937. Were you there?

This is Keynsham's entry for a competition to design a flying machine – pedal powered! Did they win a prize?

The 1st Keynsham troop taking a photo call at Winford Camp in 1995. We know that Scouts must 'Be Prepared', but a bomb found in part of their grounds (now a car park) in July 1961 took everyone by surprise. In January 2003, scouter Tim Cann delivered a Landrover to a land-mine clearing crew in south-west Bosnia (Herzegovina). The journey there and back took ten days.

Competitors from the 1st Keynsham troop took part in the Chief Scout Challenge held on Exmoor from 2 to 4 April 1993. Were you one of those awarded certificates?

We must not forget the Cub Scouts. Here they are given a special table at the annual dinner. Were you there?

Members of the Keynsham Shotokai Karate Club practice in the Memorial Park very early in the morning – 5.30 a.m. At the front of the group are Zoe Reeeves and (clockwise) Hanna Lord, Peter Lord, Kate Jones, Andrew Denn, Peter Holland and Brendon Moorhouse.

Opposite above: An exhibition and reception were held to launch the Keynsham and North Wansdyke Heritage Trust in Keynsham Parish Hall on 10 April 1987. The official party included, from left to right: Dr Peter Roberts (chairman of the trust), John Palser (town crier), Councillor Jean Pitt (chairman of Avon County Council), Councillor R.E. Powell (chairman of Wansdyke District Council), Councillor Les Sell (chairman of leisure and amenities, Wansdyke District Council), Kenneth Hudson (a national authority on museums) and Eric Linfield (secretary of the Trust).

Opposite below: Keynsham Charlton WI Golden Jubilee celebration, 19 June 2002. From left to right: Pam Sweet, Margaret Chapman, Muriel Watts, Pat Kendall, Margaret Bailey, Trixie Lovell, Wendy Tyrrell, Pat Mardles, Jean Watts, Mary Horne, Peggy Clarke, Phyllis Ryan, Grace Emery, Brenda Hulme. Members wore costumes in red, white and blue, partook of a delicious supper and exchanged memories of the Queen's reign.

ROYAL BRITISH LEGION (KEYNSHAM) BRANCH

Service
of
Remembrance

MEMORIAL PARK GATES

Lest We Forget. Each year on Remembrance Sunday, the local branch of the Royal British Legion parades through Keynsham from St John's Church to the Memorial Park Gates to lay the poppy wreaths. Peter and Mary Buck are the current standard-bearers.